Grade 4–5 Clarinet

Improve your scales!

Paul Harris

Introduction   *2*

Grade 4
E♭ major   *4*
F major   *6*
A major   *8*
C major   *10*
D major   *12*
C minor   *14*
A minor   *16*
B minor   *18*
D minor   *20*
Chromatic on F and dominant 7th in C   *22*
Complete Grade 4 scales and arpeggios   *23*
Practice chart   *27*

Grade 5
E major   *28*
G major   *30*
A♭ major   *32*
B♭ major   *34*
E♭ major   *36*
F minor   *38*
F♯ minor   *40*
G minor   *42*
C minor   *44*
C♯ minor   *46*
Chromatic scales   *48*
Dominant and diminished 7ths   *49*
Complete Grade 5 scales and arpeggios   *50*
Practice chart   *55*

FABER *ff* MUSIC

Introduction

Scales and arpeggios are important. And if taught and learned imaginatively, they can be fun!

Improve your scales! is designed to help you approach scale learning methodically and thoughtfully. Its intention is to turn learning scales into a pleasant, positive and relevant experience by gradually building up the skills to play them through cumulative and enjoyable activities.

What *Improve Your Scales!* is about

The idea of *Improve your scales!* is to present you with lots of engaging activities that lead up to playing the scale (and arpeggio). Actually playing the scale is the last thing that you do! These activities build up an understanding (of the finger patterns, technical issues, sense of key and connections with the pieces that you play) to help make the learning of scales really relevant.

At the top of each scale is a box for you to fill in the notes of the scale, and circle the notes of the arpeggio.

Sight-reading

The studies and key pieces are also ideal opportunities to practise your sight-reading. Remember to look for any markings that will help you convey the character of the piece and to count at least one bar in.

Here are two really important **Golden Rules**:

No 1 Before practising your scales make sure that you:
- Drink some water (this helps get the brain working!)
- Relax (especially your shoulders, arms, wrists and fingers)
- Check your posture.

No 2 Always practise the scale and arpeggio of the pieces you are learning.

Why are scales important?

There are many reasons and it's important you know them:
- Scales hugely improve all aspects of your finger technique, facility and control.
- Arpeggios improve your ability to move around your instrument with ease.
- Knowing your scales and arpeggios will speed up the learning of new pieces because so much material is based on scale and arpeggio patterns, and will improve your sight reading both in dealing with technical issues and reading melodic patterns.
- Knowing your scales and arpeggios will develop your sense of key.
- Playing scales and arpeggios well and with confidence will earn good marks in exams.

Scales and exams

So it's no surprise that scales are such an important part of exams! They really do help to develop your playing. In an exam, the examiner will be listening out for:
- Evenness of pulse, rhythm and tone with no unnecessary accents
- A sense of key
- Dexterity, a prompt response and a sense of fluency
- A musical shape for each example.

Think about each of these during practice sessions. Tick them off in your mind.

E♭ major

a 12th

Fill in the notes of the scale and circle the notes of the arpeggio:

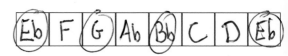

Finger fitness

In these exercises, move your fingers precisely and with energy, and not too far from the instrument.

Write the key signature of E♭ major:

> **TOP TIP** Play the *Finger fitness* exercises using different rhythms e.g. dotted rhythms.

1 □

2 □

3 □

4 □

1 □

Exams are extremely enjoyable   Scale study

2

Eccentric egghead Arpeggio study

Key piece Elegant emu

Have a go Compose or improvise a short piece using the notes
of E♭ major, beginning with these notes. Try to finish on an E♭.

You are now ready to:

☐ **say** the notes (up and down),

☐ **hear** the scale and arpeggio in your head (playing the keynote first),

☐ **think** about the finger pattern and finally,

☐ **play** the scale and arpeggio with confidence!

F major

2 octaves

Fill in the notes of the scale and circle the notes of the arpeggio:

Finger fitness

Write the key signature of F major:

> **TOP TIP** Find some examples of scale and arpeggio patterns in a piece you are learning.

1 ☐

2 ☐

3 ☐

4 ☐

1 ☐

Funny fingers Scale study

Fiesty finale Arpeggio study

Key piece Friendly fantasy

Have a go Compose or improvise a short piece using the notes
of F major, beginning with these notes. Try to finish on an F.

You are now ready to:

☐ **say** the notes (up and down),

☐ **hear** the scale and arpeggio in your head (playing the keynote first),

☐ **think** about the finger pattern and finally,

☐ **play** the scale and arpeggio with confidence!

A major

2 octaves

Fill in the notes of the scale and circle the notes of the arpeggio:

Finger fitness

Write the key signature of A major:

> **TOP TIP** Listen to the evenness of the sound as you play the *Finger fitness* exercises.

1 ☐

2 ☐

3 ☐

4 ☐

1 ☐

Alien allegro   Scale study

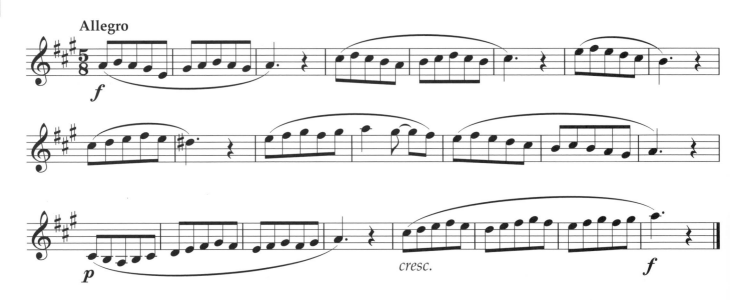

2

Amusement arcade   Duet arpeggio study

* To play in canon: Player 2 begins when Player 1 reaches this point.

Key piece   A tanker at anchor at Ankara

Have a go Compose or improvise a short piece using the notes
of A major, beginning with these notes. Try to finish on an A.

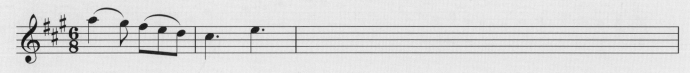

You are now ready to:

□ **say** the notes (up and down),

□ **hear** the scale and arpeggio in your head (playing the keynote first),

□ **think** about the finger pattern and finally,

□ **play** the scale and arpeggio with confidence!

C major

2 octaves

Fill in the notes of the scale and circle the notes of the arpeggio:

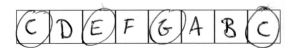

Finger fitness

Write the key signature of C major:

> **TOP TIP** Sometimes say the name of the note in your head as you play it.

Counting calories Scale study

Allegro gymnasioso

2

Crumbling cookies Arpeggio study

Key piece Circles, cylinders and coils

Have a go Compose or improvise a short piece using the notes
of C major, beginning with these notes. Try to finish on a C.

You are now ready to:

☐ **say** the notes (up and down),

☐ **hear** the scale and arpeggio in your head (playing the keynote first),

☐ **think** about the finger pattern and finally,

☐ **play** the scale and arpeggio with confidence!

D major

2 octaves

Fill in the notes of the scale and circle the notes of the arpeggio:

Finger fitness

Write the key signature of D major:

> **TOP TIP** When descending from C♯ to B across the upper break put your left-hand first finger down quickly and firmly.

Dastardly dance Scale study

Allegro con fuoco

2

Dozy dog Arpeggio study

Key piece Demonic doughnut

Have a go Compose or improvise a short piece using the notes of D major, beginning with these notes. Try to finish on a D.

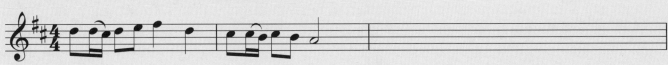

You are now ready to:

☐ **say** the notes (up and down),

☐ **hear** the scale and arpeggio in your head (playing the keynote first),

☐ **think** about the finger pattern and finally,

☐ **play** the scale and arpeggio with confidence!

C minor

a 12th

Fill in the notes of the scale and circle the notes of the arpeggio:

Finger fitness

Write the key signature of C minor:

> **TOP TIP** Put some character into your *Finger fitness* exercises. Play them gently, angrily, thoughtfully and so on.

1

2

3

4

1 **Carriage clock**   Harmonic minor scale study

2 **Courtly caper**   Melodic minor scale study

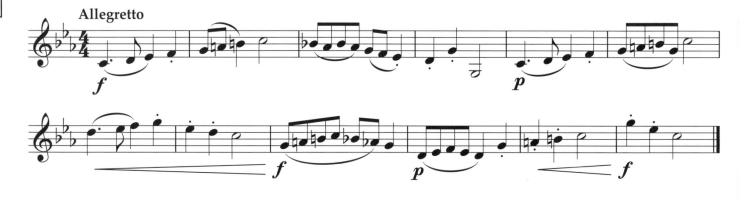

3

Carnival caprice   Arpeggio study

Key piece   Cream cake

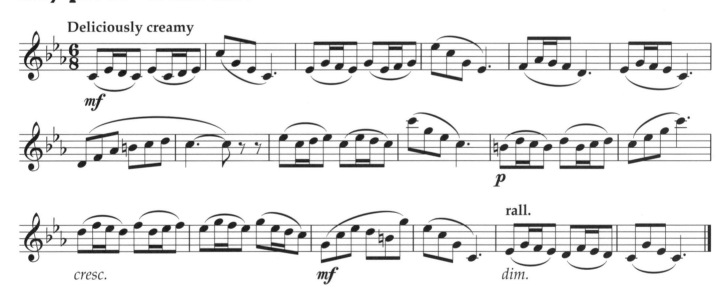

Have a go Compose or improvise a short piece using the notes
of C minor, beginning with these notes. Try to finish on a C.

You are now ready to:

- **say** the notes (up and down),
- **hear** the scale and arpeggio in your head (playing the keynote first),
- **think** about the finger pattern and finally,
- **play** the scale and arpeggio with confidence!

A minor
2 octaves

Fill in the notes of the scale and circle the notes of the arpeggio:

Finger fitness

Write the key signature of A minor:

> **TOP TIP** When moving around the throat register, keep your wrist as still as possible.

1

2

3

4

1
Abracadabra! Harmonic minor scale study

2
Arabesque Melodic minor scale study

3

Athlete   Duet arpeggio study

* To play in canon: Player 2 begins when Player 1 reaches bar 2.

Key piece   Ambling

Have a go Compose or improvise a short piece using the notes of A minor beginning, with these notes. Try to finish on an A.

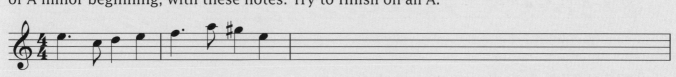

You are now ready to:

say the notes (up and down),

hear the scale and arpeggio in your head (playing the keynote first),

think about the finger pattern and finally,

play the scale and arpeggio with confidence!

B minor
2 octaves

Fill in the notes of the scale and circle the notes of the arpeggio:

Finger fitness

Write the key signature of B minor:

> **TOP TIP** Practice the *Finger fitness* exercises slurred, tongued and *staccato.*

Bazaar　Harmonic minor scale study

Moderato con moto

mf

p cresc.

rall.

f

Buccaneer　Melodic minor scale study

Swashbucklingly

mf

cresc.

f

ff

3

Boomerang Arpeggio study

Key piece **Beetroot broth**

Have a go Compose or improvise a short piece using the notes of
B minor, beginning with these notes. Try to finish on a B.

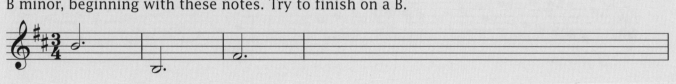

You are now ready to:

- **say** the notes (up and down),

- **hear** the scale and arpeggio in your head (playing the keynote first),

- **think** about the finger pattern and finally,

- **play** the scale and arpeggio with confidence!

D minor

2 octaves

Fill in the notes of the scale and circle the notes of the arpeggio:

Finger fitness

Write the key signature of D minor:

> **TOP TIP** When moving to C♯ across the upper break, make your finger movement vigorous and rhythmical.

1

2

3

4

Date and duck dumplings   Melodic minor scale study

1

Dashing   Harmonic minor scale study

2

As fast as possible (but not faster!)

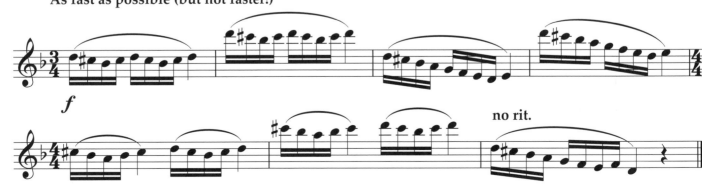

3

Dotty dalmatian   Arpeggio study

Key piece   Didgeridoo (or don't)

Have a go Compose or improvise a short piece using the notes
of D minor, beginning with these notes. Try to finish on a D.

You are now ready to:

- **say** the notes (up and down),
- **hear** the scale and arpeggio in your head (playing the keynote first),
- **think** about the finger pattern and finally,
- **play** the scale and arpeggio with confidence!

Chromatic on F and dominant 7th in C

Fiendish ferret   Chromatic starting on F

Chromatic scales move in semitone steps meaning you play
all the notes between the two key notes.

Curves and corners   Dominant 7th in the key of C

A dominant 7th is a pattern which is built on the dominant (5th note)
of the scale. It is made up of four notes: the 1st, 3rd, 5th and minor
7th above the dominant.

Complete Grade 4 scales and arpeggios

Exam requirements from the ABRSM

Scales

- E♭ major, C minor (harmonic or melodic at candidate's choice) (a 12th)
- F, A, C, D majors, A, B, D minors (harmonic or melodic at candidate's choice) (2 octaves)
- Tongued **and** slurred
- Even notes
- From memory

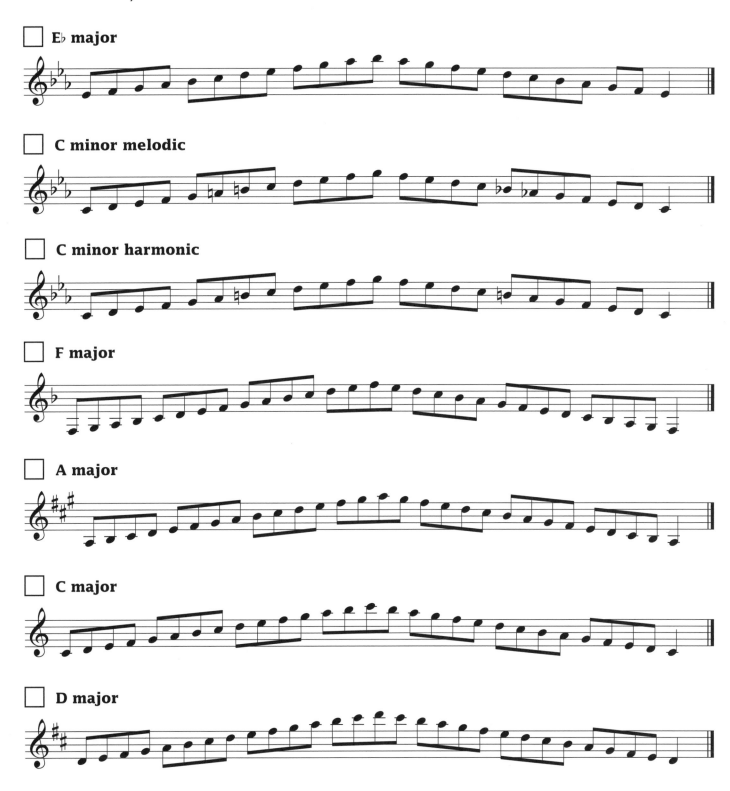

☐ **E♭ major**

☐ **C minor melodic**

☐ **C minor harmonic**

☐ **F major**

☐ **A major**

☐ **C major**

☐ **D major**

Complete Grade 4 scales and arpeggios

☐ **A minor melodic**

☐ **A minor harmonic**

☐ **B minor melodic**

☐ **B minor harmonic**

☐ **D minor melodic**

☐ **D minor harmonic**

Complete Grade 4 scales and arpeggios

Arpeggios
- E♭ major, C minor (a 12th)
- F, A, C, D majors, A, B, D minors (2 octaves)
- Tongued **and** slurred
- Even notes
- From memory

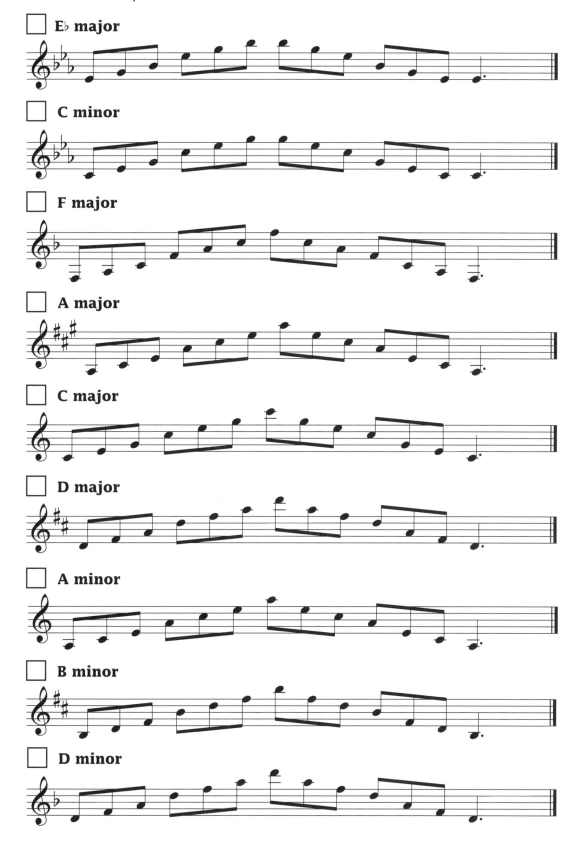

☐ **E♭ major**

☐ **C minor**

☐ **F major**

☐ **A major**

☐ **C major**

☐ **D major**

☐ **A minor**

☐ **B minor**

☐ **D minor**

Complete Grade 4 scales and arpeggios

☐ **Dominant 7th**
In the key of C

- Resolving on the tonic
- Tongued **and** slurred
- From memory

☐ **Chromatic scale**
Starting on F

- Tongued **and** slurred
- From memory

Practice chart

Fill in the chart with your chosen scales and arpeggios. Remember to practise your scales and arpeggios in different ways – with different rhythms and dynamics and thinking of different colours and flavours!

Scale/Arpeggio	Comments	Tick a box each time you practise

E major

2 octaves

Fill in the notes of the scale and circle the notes of the arpeggio:

Finger fitness

In these exercises, move your fingers precisely and with energy, and not too far from the instrument.

Write the key signature of E major:

> **TOP TIP** When playing low E, always maintain firm breath support.

Energetic earthworm   Scale study

2

Eerie eel   Arpeggio study

Slimily

mp *molto legato*

Key piece   Eezee!

Funky

mf

p   *cresc.*

f

Have a go Compose or improvise a short piece using the notes
of E major, beginning with these notes. Try to finish on an E.

You are now ready to:

☐ **say** the notes (up and down),

☐ **hear** the scale and arpeggio in your head (playing the keynote first),

☐ **think** about the finger pattern and finally,

☐ **play** the scale and arpeggio with confidence!

G major

2 octaves

Fill in the notes of the scale and circle the notes of the arpeggio:

Finger fitness

Write the key signature of G major:

> **TOP TIP** Sometimes visualise the next fingering before you make it.

Gossamer   Scale study

2

Gallant galley Arpeggio study

Key piece **Georgian gallop**

Have a go Compose or improvise a short piece using the notes
of G major, beginning with these notes. Try to finish on a G.

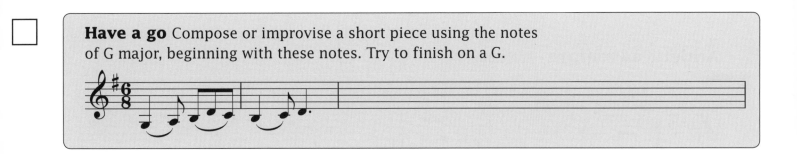

You are now ready to:

- **say** the notes (up and down),
- **hear** the scale and arpeggio in your head (playing the keynote first),
- **think** about the finger pattern and finally,
- **play** the scale and arpeggio with confidence!

C → F → Bb → Eb → Ab

Ab major

2 octaves

Fill in the notes of the scale and circle the notes of the arpeggio:

Finger fitness

Write the key signature of Ab major:

> **TOP TIP** Try playing the *Finger fitness* exercises in swung rhythms.

1

2

3

4

Athletic adventure Scale study

1

2

Amorous arpeggios   Arpeggio study

Key piece   Allemande

Have a go Compose or improvise a short piece using the notes
of Ab major, beginning with these notes. Try to finish on an Ab.

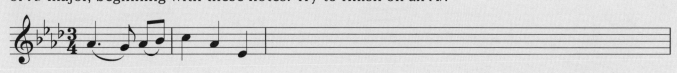

You are now ready to:

say the notes (up and down),

hear the scale and arpeggio in your head (playing the keynote first),

think about the finger pattern and finally,

play the scale and arpeggio with confidence!

B♭ major

2 octaves

Fill in the notes of the scale and circle the notes of the arpeggio:

Bb C D Eb F G A Bb

Finger fitness

Write the key signature of B♭ major:

> **TOP TIP** Work carefully on coordinating fingers when moving from E♭ to F in both registers.

1   70 80 90 100 110 130 140

2   70 80 90 100 110 130 140

3   60 70 85 95 110 120

4   60 70 80 100

1 **Bilberry blossom**   Scale study

Delicately ♩. = 65

f

mp   *dim.*   *p*

f   *rit.*

2

Blizzard Arpeggio study

Key piece Don't be flat, be natural

Have a go Compose or improvise a short piece using the notes of B♭ major, beginning with these notes. Try to finish on a B♭.

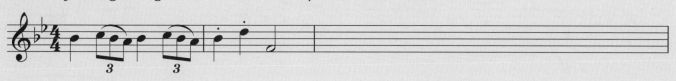

You are now ready to:

☐ **say** the notes (up and down),

☐ **hear** the scale and arpeggio in your head (playing the keynote first),

☐ **think** about the finger pattern and finally,

☐ **play** the scale and arpeggio with confidence!

E♭ major

2 octaves

Fill in the notes of the scale and circle the notes of the arpeggio:

Finger fitness

Write the key signature of E♭ major:

> **TOP TIP** Remember to support the high notes with lots of fast air.

2

Elf Arpeggio study

Allegretto leggiero

mf sempre staccato

f   *dim.*   *p*

Player 2
(*ad lib.*)

Key piece Eucalyptus

Andante espressivo

mp

f

mp

Have a go Compose or improvise a short piece using the notes
of Eᵇ major, beginning with these notes. Try to finish on an Eᵇ.

You are now ready to:

☐ **say** the notes (up and down),

☐ **hear** the scale and arpeggio in your head (playing the keynote first),

☐ **think** about the finger pattern and finally,

☐ **play** the scale and arpeggio with confidence!

F minor

2 octaves

Fill in the notes of the
scale and circle the
notes of the arpeggio:

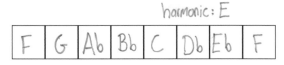

harmonic: E

| F | G | Ab | Bb | C | Db | Eb | F |

Finger fitness

Write the key signature
of F minor:

> **TOP TIP** Try to hear the *Finger fitness* exercises in your
> head before you play them.

75   80

1

60

2

3

4

1

Fiendish fox   Scale study

Allegro con fuoco

f   E Db C Bb Ab G   *mp*

cresc.   C Bb Ab G LH   *mf*

rit.   *a tempo*

ff   *sfz*

2

Funky Arpeggio study

Key piece Finale fantastique

Have a go Compose or improvise a short piece using the notes
of F minor, beginning with these notes. Try to finish on an F.

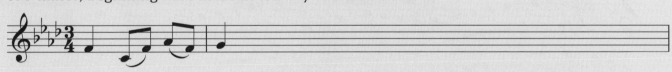

You are now ready to:

☐ **say** the notes (up and down),

☐ **hear** the scale and arpeggio in your head (playing the keynote first),

☐ **think** about the finger pattern and finally,

☐ **play** the scale and arpeggio with confidence!

F♯ minor

2 octaves

Fill in the notes of the scale and circle the notes of the arpeggio:

Finger fitness

Write the key signature of F♯ minor:

> **TOP TIP** Once you have played a *Finger fitness* exercise a few times, try it faster! And then even faster!

Frisky fingers   Scale study

* This study is based on the harmonic minor scale. How could you adapt it to use the melodic minor scale?

2

Fives fantasy   Arpeggio study

Key piece   Funny fellow

Have a go Compose or improvise a short piece using the notes
of F♯ minor, beginning with these notes. Try to finish on an F♯.

You are now ready to:

☐ **say** the notes (up and down),

☐ **hear** the scale and arpeggio in your head (playing the keynote first),

☐ **think** about the finger pattern and finally,

☐ **play** the scale and arpeggio with confidence!

G minor

2 octaves

Fill in the notes of the
scale and circle the
notes of the arpeggio:

| G | A | Bb | C | D | Eb | F# | G |

Finger fitness

Write the key signature
of G minor:

> **TOP TIP** Practise each exercise, four notes at a time. Play
> these notes with really precise fingering, then play the
> whole exercise continuously.

Gherkin gateau   Scale study

2

Gargling gargoyle Arpeggio study

Key piece Ghastly gigue

Have a go Compose or improvise a short piece using the notes of G minor, beginning with these notes. Try to finish on a G.

You are now ready to:

- [ ] **say** the notes (up and down),
- [ ] **hear** the scale and arpeggio in your head (playing the keynote first),
- [ ] **think** about the finger pattern and finally,
- [ ] **play** the scale and arpeggio with confidence!

C minor

2 octaves

Fill in the notes of the scale and circle the notes of the arpeggio:

Finger fitness

Write the key signature of C minor:

> **TOP TIP** Try adding some *staccato* and accented notes to the *Finger fitness* exercises.

Crème caramel   Scale study

* This study is based on the melodic minor scale. How could you adapt it to make use of the harmonic minor scale?

2

Crusty crumpet Arpeggio study

Swung and very cool

Key piece Cantering camel

Vivo

Have a go Compose or improvise a short piece using the notes
of C minor, beginning with these notes. Try to finish on a C.

You are now ready to:

- [ ] **say** the notes (up and down),
- [ ] **hear** the scale and arpeggio in your head (playing the keynote first),
- [ ] **think** about the finger pattern and finally,
- [ ] **play** the scale and arpeggio with confidence!

C♯ minor
2 octaves

Fill in the notes of the scale and circle the notes of the arpeggio:

Finger fitness

Write the key signature of C♯ minor:

> **TOP TIP** For best results, repeat each *Finger fitness* exercise at least four times.

1

2

3

4

1

Cheese 'n' chilli   Scale study

2

Carrot cake   Arpeggio study

Key piece   Cool as a cucumber

Have a go Compose or improvise a short piece using the notes
of C# minor, beginning with these notes. Try to finish on a C#.

You are now ready to:

- **say** the notes (up and down),
- **hear** the scale and arpeggio in your head (playing the keynote first),
- **think** about the finger pattern and finally,
- **play** the scale and arpeggio with confidence!

Chromatic scales

Chromatic scales move in semitone steps, meaning you play
all the notes between the two key notes.

1

Cretaceous carnivore   Chromatic starting on C

2

Action movie   Chromatic starting on A

Dominant and diminished 7ths

A dominant 7th is a pattern which is built on the dominant (5th note) of the scale.
It is made up of four notes: the 1st, 3rd, 5th and minor 7th above the dominant.

1

Fishing boat   Dominant 7th in the key of F

2

Dance of the dazzling duchess   Dominant 7th in the key of D

3

Grizzly   Diminished 7th starting on G

A diminished 7th is a pattern of four notes that spans the interval of nine semitones
(a diminished 7th). Each interval is a minor 3rd (which is sometimes written as an
augmented 2nd, so they may look like next door notes).

Complete Grade 5 scales and arpeggios

Exam requirements from the ABRSM

Scales

• E, G, A♭, B♭, E♭ majors, F, F♯, G, C, C♯ minors (harmonic or melodic at candidate's choice) (2 octaves)
• Tongued **and** slurred
• Even notes
• From memory

☐ **E major**

☐ **G major**

☐ **A♭ major**

☐ **B♭ major**

☐ **E♭ major**

☐ **F minor melodic**

☐ **F minor harmonic**

Complete Grade 5 scales and arpeggios

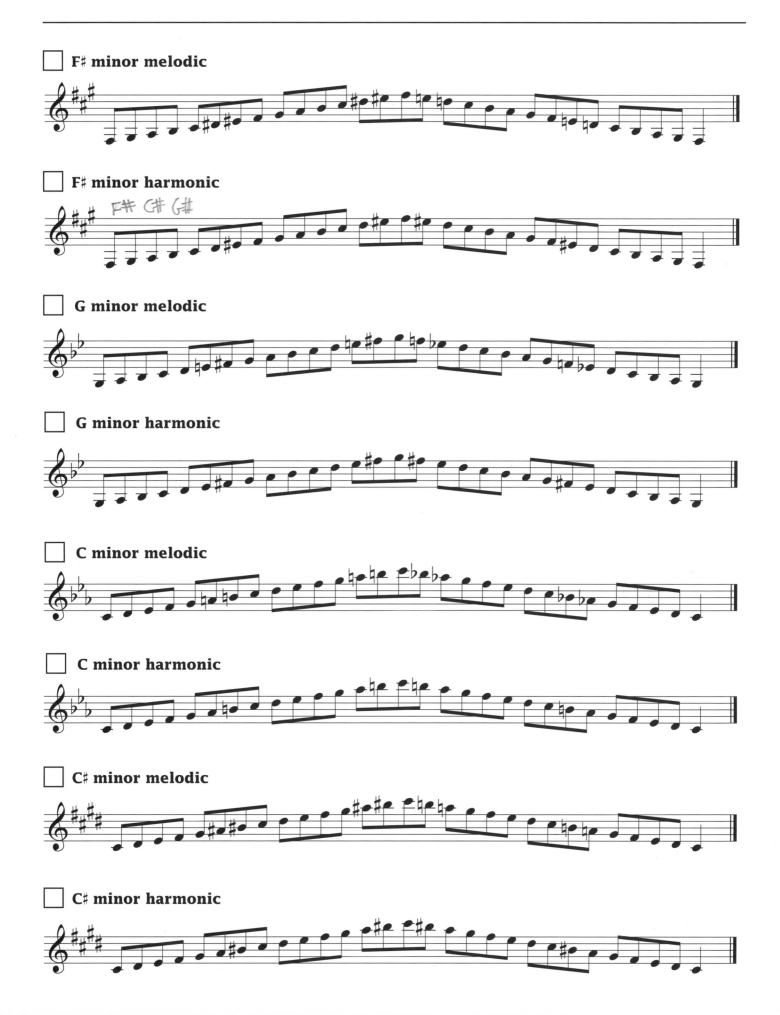

☐ **F♯ minor melodic**

☐ **F♯ minor harmonic**

F# C# G#

☐ **G minor melodic**

☐ **G minor harmonic**

☐ **C minor melodic**

☐ **C minor harmonic**

☐ **C♯ minor melodic**

☐ **C♯ minor harmonic**

Complete Grade 5 scales and arpeggios

Arpeggios

- E, G, A♭, B♭, E♭ majors, F, F♯, G, C, C♯ minors (2 octaves)
- Tongued **and** slurred
- Even notes
- From memory

☐ **E major**

☐ **G major**

☐ **A♭ major**

☐ **B♭ major**

☐ **E♭ major**

☐ **F minor**

☐ **F♯ minor**

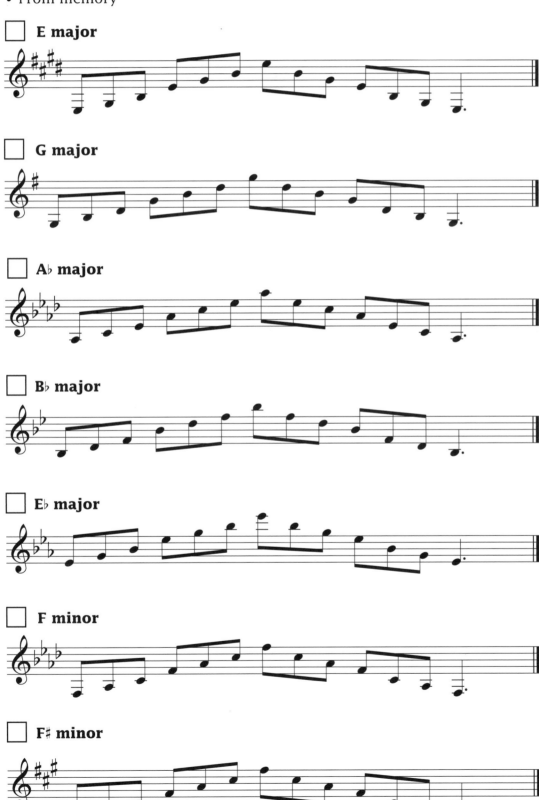

Complete Grade 5 scales and arpeggios

☐ **G minor**

☐ **C minor**

☐ **C♯ minor**

Dominant 7ths
- Resolving on the tonic
- Tongued **and** slurred
- From memory

☐ **In the key of D**

☐ **In the key of F**

Diminished 7ths
- Tongued **and** slurred
- From memory

☐ **Starting on G**

Complete Grade 5 scales and arpeggios

Chromatic scales
- Tongued **and** slurred
- From memory

☐ **Starting on A**

☐ **Starting on C**